the facts about
FORCES
and MOTION

Rebecca Hunter

W
FRANKLIN WATTS
LONDON·SYDNEY

© Franklin Watts 2003

First published in 2003 by
Franklin Watts
96 Leonard Street
London
EC2A 4XD

Franklin Watts Australia
45-51 Huntley Street
Alexandria
NSW 2015

ISBN: 0-7496-4878-3

A CIP catalogue record for this book is available from
the British Library

Printed in Hong Kong, China
Planning and production by Discovery Books Limited
Editor: Rebecca Hunter
Design: Keith Williams
Consultant: Jeremy Bloomfield
Illustrations: Stefan Chabluk: page 16; Keith Williams:
page 21, page 22, page 26, page 27.

Photographs:
Bruce Coleman: cover, page 5, page 8 (Christer
Fredriksson), page 9 top, page 11, page 12, page 17,
page 22, page 29 (Jeff Foott); Corbis: page 14, page 16;
Discovery Picture Library: page 4, page 19 top, page 20
bottom, page 28 bottom; Impact Photos: page 7
(Ken Graham); Mary Evans Picture Library: page 18;
NASA: page 13, page 28; Oxford Scientific Films: page
10 (Bernd Schellhammer), page 15 (Laurence Gould), page
25 (Alain Christof); Photodisc: page 9 bottom; Rebecca
Hunter: page 6, page 19 bottom; Science Photo Library:
page 20 top (Richard Megna), page 23 (Cordelia Molloy),
page 24 (James Stevenson), page 27 (John Howard), page
28 right.

the facts about
FORCES
and MOTION

Contents

Words in **bold** appear in the glossary on page 30.

What is a force?

A force is a push or a pull. You cannot see forces but you can see the effect they have on things.

A force makes something move. Once an object starts moving, it will keep moving until another force stops it. There are four ways in which forces act on things: they can make them speed up, slow down, change direction or change shape.

Speeding up and slowing down

If you are riding a bicycle and want to go faster, you have to pedal harder. You use more force, which makes you speed up. When you want to slow down you use the brakes. These produce a force of **friction** which slows the wheels. The bicycle will slow down and eventually stop.

Changing direction

When you hit a ball you use force to change the way it is moving. A tennis player hits a ball that is moving towards them. The ball then changes direction and moves away from them.

A twisting movement is a force that makes something rotate. When you need to open a jar, you twist the lid one way. Twisting it the opposite way closes it.

Changing shape

A force can also change the shape of something. Squashing or stretching things can alter their shape. Some things squash or stretch more easily than others.

► These yachts have many forces working on them, including both **upthrust** from the water and the movement of the wind.

It is easy to stretch elastic or squash a sponge. It is not easy to squash or stretch wood or iron or steel. Steel can only be stretched if it is made into a spring. When springs are pulled by a force they stretch. When the force is removed, the spring returns to its original shape.

There are other forces at work around us too. Boats float because of the force of water pushing upwards. **Compasses** work because of the force of **magnetism**. The force of friction makes things grip. We stay on the surface of the Earth because of the force of **gravity**. You will find out about all these forces in this book.

key facts

- A force is a push or pull.
- Forces make things speed up, slow down, change direction or change shape.
- Friction, magnetism and gravity are all forces.

5

Friction

Friction is a force that occurs when two surfaces rub against each other.

When this happens the two surfaces stick to each other a little – they grip each other. This grip slows the movement down.

If you push a toy car along the floor, it will start off travelling fast, but will soon slow down and stop. This is due to the force of friction between the car's wheels and the floor.

The amount of friction depends on the type of surface. Rough surfaces slow things down quicker so we say the friction between them is greater. Smooth surfaces slide over each other easily – the amount of friction between them is small.

Useful friction

Friction is a very useful force. Without it you would not be able to pick anything up: things would just slide out of your hands. People would fall over, and cars and aeroplanes would not be able to stop!

We make use of friction all the time. Outdoor shoes have deep treads on the sole so you can walk safely on slippery, wet pavements or climb muddy hills without falling over. The deeper the tread the more the shoe grips the ground.

▼ A tractor needs large tyres with deep treads to give it a good grip on a ploughed field.

Cars have treads on their tyres to give them good grip on wet roads. It is dangerous to drive when the tread has worn down.

Sometimes we want to reduce friction as much as possible to allow things to go faster. Skiers polish their skis to make them as smooth as possible so they can move quickly over the snow.

▼ There is very little friction between skis and snow, enabling skiers to move very fast.

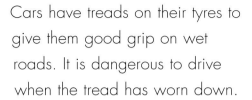

Friction and heat

Friction produces heat. You can prove this yourself by rubbing your hands together. They will soon feel warm.

Sometimes the heat produced by friction can be a nuisance or even dangerous. Most machines have moving parts. They are usually covered in oil and grease to reduce friction. Without this, the parts would soon wear out and, in some cases, the heat produced by friction could start a fire.

key facts

○ Friction acts when two surfaces touch each other.

○ Friction slows things down.

○ Friction gives us grip.

○ Friction produces heat.

Air and water resistance

Things that move are slowed down not only by the surface they move on (friction) but by the substance they pass through. Both air and water create drag or resistance.

When a leaf falls from a tree, it doesn't plunge straight down as a stone would, it floats gently. This is because air is pushing up against the surface of the leaf. The bigger the **surface area**, the greater the air resistance. A big leaf encounters more air resistance than a small one and therefore takes longer to fall.

▶ Paragliders make use of air resistance to slow their fall.
The open canopy has a very large surface area so it encounters a lot of air resistance.

Streamlining

If you want something to travel fast through the air, it must be streamlined. This means it has a smooth, slim shape that offers the least resistance to the air. Rockets, aeroplanes, arrows and bullets all have streamlined shapes and can travel at very high speeds.

Birds also need to move easily through the air. If you look at the shape of fast-moving birds such as swallows or hawks you can see how they are streamlined. Most flightless birds do not need to be streamlined. An ostrich is obviously not designed to fly!

◀ A jet boat is designed to move as fast as possible over water.

Water resistance

Water creates a greater resistance than air, so to move through water you also need to be streamlined. Speedboats are pointed and smooth so they can move fast over the water. Although a rowing dinghy is not built for speed, it still needs a pointed bow to be able to move across the water.

Animals that live in the water often have very similar shapes. If you compare the shapes of a dolphin (mammal), a shark (fish) and a penguin (bird), they are all very similar. Their shape enables them to move fast and easily underwater.

key facts

- Air resistance slows things down.
- Water resistance is greater than air resistance.
- Streamlined objects can move faster through the air and through water.

Gravity

Gravity is the force that keeps you on the ground. Without gravity you would fly off into space!

Gravity pulls everything towards the centre of the Earth. It is the force that makes things fall when they are dropped. When you throw a ball in the air your throw pushes the ball upwards. The force of your throw only takes the ball so high. The pull of gravity slows the ball down and it is pulled back to the ground. All things on Earth are affected by gravity. It affects things in the air, in water and on the ground.

Weight

Heavy objects are pulled strongly towards the centre of the Earth by gravity. A light object is not being pulled as strongly. Gravity pulling down on an object gives it weight.

However, things that are the same size do not always weigh the same: big things are not necessarily heavier than small things. A balloon is much lighter than a watermelon of the same size. A television set is smaller, but much heavier, than an inflated air bed. This makes it difficult to judge the weight of something just by looking at it.

▶ What goes up must come down! A BMX biker makes use of gravity to give a spectacular display.

Discovering gravity

You might think that heavier things fall to Earth faster than light things. However, four hundred years ago an Italian scientist named Galileo did an experiment to show that, if you ignore air resistance, all things fall at the same speed whatever their weight. So if a large bowling ball and a small golf ball were dropped off a tall building at the same time they would reach the ground at the same time. The only thing that can interfere with this rule is air resistance which, as we have seen (page 8), acts on things with a large surface area and slows them down.

▲ A pole vaulter needs to use her strength and skills of balance to overcome the force of gravity and get over the bar.

key facts

- Gravity pulls all things towards the centre of the Earth.
- Gravity gives things weight.
- All things fall at the same speed.

Gravity outside the Earth

Gravity is a force that attracts all objects to each other. The bigger the object, the greater its gravitational force.

In the 17th century, the British scientist Isaac Newton realized that the force that makes things fall to Earth was the same force that keeps the Moon **orbiting** the Earth and the planets going round the Sun.

Scientists have proved that gravity exists between all the immense objects in space — between stars and between the planets, moons and **asteroids**.

Escaping gravity

The strength of gravitational force is the same all over the Earth. It takes a very powerful force and a lot of speed (called the escape velocity) in order to transport people and machines beyond the pull of the Earth's gravity.

▼ All the planets in our solar system are held in place around the Sun by the force of the Sun's gravity.

The space shuttle is almost 31 times more powerful than a Boeing 747 jumbo jet; it accelerates to 28,000 kph to get into orbit above the Earth's atmosphere.

Gravity on the Moon

Because the Moon is much smaller than the Earth, its force of gravity is much less. It is actually one sixth of the gravity of Earth. This means that the weight of everything on the Moon is one sixth of what it would be on Earth. The space suits that astronauts wear in space feel really heavy on Earth. On the Moon they feel almost weightless.

The world's long jump record is 8.95m on Earth. On the Moon it could be as much as 54m! Jupiter, the largest planet in our solar system, has a much stronger pull of gravity than Earth. On Jupiter the jump would not be more than 3.4m.

▲ There is little gravity on the Moon and astronauts feel almost weightless. The space suits that seem so cumbersome on Earth become much easier to wear on the Moon.

key facts

- The force of gravity exists in space between stars and planets.

- The Earth is kept in orbit around the Sun by the Sun's force of gravity.

- The force of gravity is much weaker on the Moon because it is smaller than the Earth.

Upthrust

When something pushes down on water, the water pushes up. The force of water pushing back is called upthrust.

Upthrust is also produced in air, but it is much greater in water. You can feel the upthrust when you try to push a beach ball under the water. When an object is put in water it weighs much less than when it is in the air. This is because the upthrust of the water cancels out some of the force of gravity pulling down.

▼ The upthrust of water keeps this dinghy, and the children, on the surface of the water.

You can do it...

Prove how upthrust works. Take a blob of plasticine and drop it in a sink of water. It will sink. Now make the plasticine into the shape of a bowl. Put it into the water again. If it still doesn't float you will need to make the surface area even greater; flatten it out a bit more.

Sinking and floating

An object in water has at least two forces acting on it. Gravity is pulling it down and giving it weight, and upthrust is pushing it up. The force of the upthrust depends on how much water has been pushed out of the way by the object. We say this is the amount of water it displaces. A large object displaces a lot of water so the upthrust is big. If only a small amount of water is displaced the upthrust will be smaller than the force of gravity.

The combination of upthrust and weight determines whether an object will sink or float in water. When the upthrust is equal to or greater than the weight, an object will float. If the weight is greater than the upthrust, the object will sink.

▲ Anchors are designed to sink and hold a boat in place. They are made of metal and their weight is much greater than the upthrust of water.

key facts

○ The force of water pushing up is called upthrust.

○ Upthrust is greater in water than in air.

○ The size of upthrust in water depends on the amount of water displaced.

○ When upthrust is equal to or greater than its weight, the object will float.

Forces in motion

Everywhere you look there are objects in motion.

Birds and aeroplanes fly overhead, cars move along roads, people run or walk, trees move in the wind, rivers flow downhill. Forces act on all things to make them move. Once they are moving, they will continue to move until another force makes them alter speed, change direction or stop.

▲ The sledge will carry on moving until friction finally makes it stop.

Size and direction

A force has two parts, size and direction. These can be shown in diagrams with arrows. The stronger the force, the greater the movement.

Combining forces

Many objects are acted on by more than one force. Sometimes forces combine to create one, bigger force. For example, when two horses are harnessed together to pull a cart, they each create a forward force. These two forces combine together to produce one large forward force.

◀ Here a ball has been passed to a footballer with a small force. When he kicks the ball he applies a larger force and changes the direction of the ball.

▲ This sailing boat is staying upright because the weight of the crew balances the force of the wind in the sails.

Balanced forces

If an object is still, it doesn't mean there are no forces acting on it. Forces are always in action. If nothing happens when a force acts on an object, it means that the force must be balanced by another force pushing in the opposite direction. We say they are in **equilibrium**.

If the two teams in a tug-of-war are equal in number and strength, the rope will not move: the two forces cancel each other out and produce a balance. If someone else joins one of the teams, that team will now be stronger. It will exert a stronger force and probably win the contest.

key facts

- Forces have two parts: size and direction.

- To make something move, one force must be stronger than another.

- If two forces are equal, they are balanced and the object will not move.

A tent is an example of several forces in equilibrium. The guy ropes and tent pegs at one end pull in opposite directions to those at the other end. Gravity is also pulling the tent downwards. As long as the poles and ropes remain in place, the tent will stay up.

Measuring forces

Force is measured in units called **newtons**. The newton is named after Sir Isaac Newton, who was one of the first people who really understood the force of gravity.

We use an instrument called a forcemeter to measure how strong a force is. A forcemeter has a spring inside it. As the spring is stretched, a marker moves along a scale, which indicates the size of the stretching force. The scale shows the force in newtons. Forces of up to 100 newtons can be measured using a forcemeter.

One newton is the force needed to lift a small apple. When you kick a ball, the kick applies a force of about 10 newtons.

◄ Sir Isaac Newton (1642-1727) was one of the world's greatest scientists. He developed his ideas about gravity after watching an apple fall from a tree in his orchard.

▼ The force of a jet engine is 100,000 newtons.

Weight and gravity

A set of weighing scales works in the same way as a forcemeter. It is used to measure the pull of gravity on an object. When you put something on the scales, you are actually measuring the pull of gravity on it. The scale tells us the object's weight in grams and kilograms.

key facts

○ The unit of force, the newton, is named after Sir Isaac Newton.

○ Force is measured with a forcemeter.

○ The force of gravity gives things weight.

Magnetism

Magnetism is another invisible force that is easy to see in action. Magnetism is the ability of a piece of metal to attract something to it or push something away from it.

A magnet is a piece of metal that will attract another metal. Metals that contain iron are attracted to magnets and are said to be magnetic. Nickel is also magnetic.

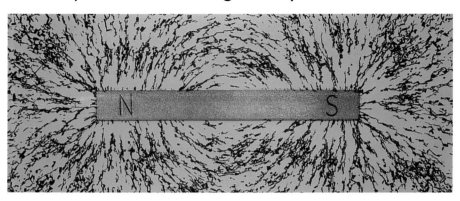

▲ The effect of the magnetic field around a bar magnet can be seen if you sprinkle **iron filings** around the magnet. The iron filings always arrange themselves into the same kind of pattern.

Magnetic poles

All magnets have two ends or poles. These are called north and south poles. They are sometimes marked on a magnet with the letters N and S. Some magnets are painted so that the north pole is red and the south pole is blue. The north pole of a magnet is always attracted to the south pole of another. Two north or two south poles will push away from, or repel, each other. The area around a magnet where its magnetic force can be detected is called a magnetic field.

▲ Bar magnet   ▲ Round magnet   ▲ Horseshoe magnet

▲ Magnets come in many shapes and sizes. Fridge magnets are the most commonly seen around the house.

Making magnets

Some magnets keep their magnetism all the time. They are called permanent magnets. Other metals can be made into magnets for a short time. This is because a magnetic metal can be thought of as containing millions of tiny magnets. In a magnet these are all facing the same way so their magnetism combines as one large magnet. In a non-magnetized metal, they face in different directions so that their magnetism cancels out. It is possible to line the tiny magnets up in a piece of iron or steel and so make a magnet.

▼ Magnetized metal

▼ Non-magnetized metal

You can do it...

Make a magnet. Stroke a steel nail with a magnet. Always stroke it with the same end of the magnet, and always stroke in the same direction down the nail. Stroke the nail about 30 times. Now hold the nail over some paper clips. How many will it pick up? If you stroke the nail some more you will make it more magnetic, and it will pick up more paper clips.

key facts

- Magnetism is a force between two magnetic materials.

- Magnets are attracted to certain metals.

- Anything that contains iron will be attracted to a magnet.

Magnetic Earth

Because the centre of the Earth is made of iron, the Earth acts like a giant magnet.

Like a magnet, Earth has two magnetic poles. One of these is close to the North Pole. This is called the magnetic north pole. The magnetic south pole is near the South Pole.

The fact that the Earth acts like a giant magnet and has its own magnetic field can be very useful for travellers. This is because any magnet that is allowed to move freely will line itself up so that it points in a north-south direction.

▲ There are many different sorts of compass for use on land, at sea and underwater.

▲ The Earth's magnetic field is similar in shape to that produced by a magnet and iron filings (see page 20).

Magnetic compass

A compass consists of a magnetic needle that is balanced so that it swings freely. The needle's south pole points towards the Earth's magnetic north pole. This enables travellers to know which direction is north and therefore which way to go. A compass is especially useful to ships at sea. Since there are no landmarks at sea, sailors rely on a compass to help them **navigate**.

You can do it...

Make your own compass. Make a needle act like a magnet by stroking it with a magnet (see page 21). Then float the needle on a piece of cork or polystyrene in a bowl of water. The needle will swing around and point in a north-south direction.

Lodestone

Magnetite is a type of iron ore that is often magnetic. It used to be called lodestone, which means 'guiding stone', and was used by sailors as a compass over 1,000 years ago.

key facts

- Because of its iron centre the Earth acts like a giant magnet.

- A compass always points north-south.

- Lodestone is a natural magnet that was used as an early type of compass.

Living with forces

We have to cope with forces every day of our lives. Because we cannot change them, we have to learn to live with them, and use them for our own benefit.

Often we have to find the right balance between forces. When you learn to ride a bicycle, you have to cope with the forces of gravity, friction and air resistance. The force you apply to the pedals drives you forward. If there were no force of friction, you would not be able to move forward and your wheels would just spin and not grip the ground.

If it was a windy day and the force of air resistance was greater than your forward force, you would be blown backwards. Or else the force of gravity would pull you to the ground! Fortunately your forward force is usually greater than air resistance, friction and gravity, and you are usually able to move in the direction you want.

Forces in buildings

When architects and engineers design buildings and bridges they have to take account of the forces that will be acting on them. If the **foundations** and walls are not strong enough, the structures will bend or fall down.

◀ In parts of the world where **earthquakes** are common, building earthquake-resistant buildings can be quite a challenge. This triangular building in San Francisco has been designed to resist earthquakes.

▲ The Pont du Gard in France was built by the Romans in 19 BCE as an **aqueduct** to carry water to Nîmes. Thanks to its strong arches, it is still standing 2,000 years later.

The triangle is the strongest shape to build with and is used in the construction of many buildings and bridges. An arch is almost as strong as a triangle. Because it is both strong and decorative, it can be found in many large buildings, tunnels and bridges.

key facts

- Engineers have to take forces into account when designing buildings.

- Triangles are the strongest shapes to build with.

- Buildings can be designed to withstand the forces caused by earthquakes.

Making forces work for us

There are many ways in which forces can be made to work for us. Simple machines work on the principle of using a small force to make a large one.

Levers

If you want to move an object such as a large rock that is too heavy to move on your own, it is often possible to do it by using a lever. A lever is a long rod propped up on a small object, called a fulcrum. When you push down on the rod at the end furthest from the fulcrum, a greater force is produced at the other end and this raises the **load**.

Wheel and axle

In a wheel and axle device, a wheel is used to turn an axle which can be used to raise a load. An example of this is the winch system that pulls a bucket out of a well. The handle (the wheel) turns a shaft (the axle) which is attached to a rope and bucket. The winch will lift the load with a greater force than the effort needed to turn the handle.

▼ A lever

Lever

PUSH

Fulcrum

Load

▼ A wheel and axle

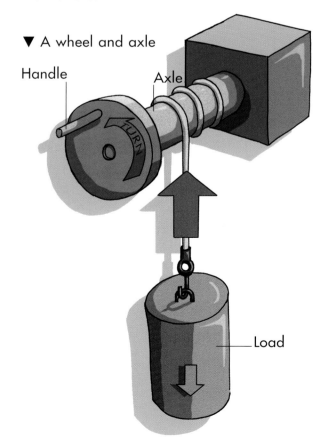

Handle

Axle

TURN

Load

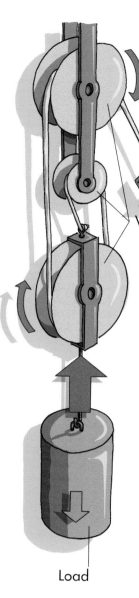

◄ A pulley

Wheels

Load

Pulleys

Another way to lift a heavy load is with a pulley system. This consists of a set of wheels with a rope wound between them. One end of the rope is attached to the load. The other is pulled by a person. The more wheels there are in the pulley system, the easier it is to lift the load.

Gears

Gears are toothed wheels that are locked together in pairs. They can **magnify** speed or force to a greater or lesser extent depending on the size of the wheels and the number of teeth. You can see gear wheels at work inside watches and clocks but they are present in many larger machines too.

Forces around us

Forces are needed to start things moving, to change the way they move, and to stop them moving. Without forces and energy, nothing would happen.

The **atmosphere** of a planet or star is kept in place by the force of gravity. The Earth's force of gravity holds all of us on the surface of the planet.

A moving object will continue to move until the friction produced by air or water resistance slows it down, and then eventually it will stop.

▼ Magnetism is an invisible force between metal objects. This magnetic sculpture shows how the force of magnetism works on metals containing iron.

▲ A huge amount of energy is needed to launch a rocket into space. This energy is obtained from the rocket's fuel and is converted into an enormous upward force.

key facts

- The world is full of forces.
- Forces make things move.
- Forces can push things apart or hold things together.
- Moving objects have more than one force acting on them.
- The force of gravity holds everything on the planet.
- Friction is a force that causes objects to slow down and stop.
- Magnetism is an invisible force between certain metals.

There is always more than one force acting on any moving object. What happens to the object depends on which force is strongest. In this picture, the boat is floating because the force of the upthrust of water is greater than the weight of the boat's gravity. The boat is moving forward because the force of movement made by the canoeist is greater than the force of friction the water resistance creates.

Glossary

Aqueduct A bridge-like structure built to carry water, usually across a valley.

Asteroid A rocky body that orbits the Sun.

Atmosphere A layer of gases that surrounds the Earth.

Compass A device that shows the direction of north.

Earthquake A major shaking of the Earth.

Equilibrium When two things are in a state of balance.

Foundations The part of a building that is underground.

Friction A force which slows down or stops the movement of one surface against another.

Generate To make or create.

Gravity The force of attraction between two masses. It attracts all things to Earth and give them weight.

Iron filings Small shavings of iron.

Load An object that needs to be moved or carried.

Magnetism The invisible force of attraction between some substances especially iron. The substance is said to be magnetic.

Magnify To make bigger.

Navigate To find one's way to a destination.

Newton Force is measured in units called newtons.

Orbiting The way in which a planet or satellite goes around another body, such as a star or a planet.

Surface area The area of the outside of something.

Upthrust The upward push on an object in water.

Further information

Books

Forces & Simple Machines (Science Factory)
Jon Richards,
Franklin Watts 2002

Magnets (Science Factory)
Jon Richards,
Franklin Watts 2002

Magnets (Science Experiments)
Sally Nankivell-Aston,
Franklin Watts 1999

Forces and Movement (Straightforward Science)
Peter Riley,
Franklin Watts 1998

Websites

Beginner's Guide to Aerodynamics
Learn about the study of forces and the resulting motion of objects through the air. Includes problems to try and an index of topics from NASA.
http://www.lerc.nasa.gov/WWW/K-12/airplane/bga.html

Funderstanding Roller Coaster
How high or fast can you go? Design your own coaster and achieve maximum thrills and chills without crashing or flying off the track by learning about force, friction and gravity.
http://www.funderstanding.com/k12/coaster/

Newton's Laws of Motion
Discover more about Newton and his laws of motion.
http://id.mind.net/~zona/mstm/physics/mechanics/forces/newton/newton.html

Physics4Kids
Find out how physics is a part of everything we know! This site has simple explanations of motion, thermodynamics, light, modern physics and electricity.
http://www.kapili.com/topiclist.html

Places to Visit

UK
The Science Museum
Exhibition Road, South Kensington,
London SW7 2DD

Museum of Science and Industry
Castlefield, Manchester M3 4FP

Glasgow Science Centre
50 Pacific Quay, Glasgow G51 1EA, Scotland

Techniquest
Stuart Street, Cardiff CF10 5BW, Wales

Australia
Australian Museum
6 College Street, Sydney NSW 2010

Scitech Discovery Centre
City West, Railway Parade, West Perth

Questacon
The National Science and Technology Centre
King Edward Terrace, Canberra ACT 2000

New Zealand
Otago Museum
Dunedin, New Zealand

Index

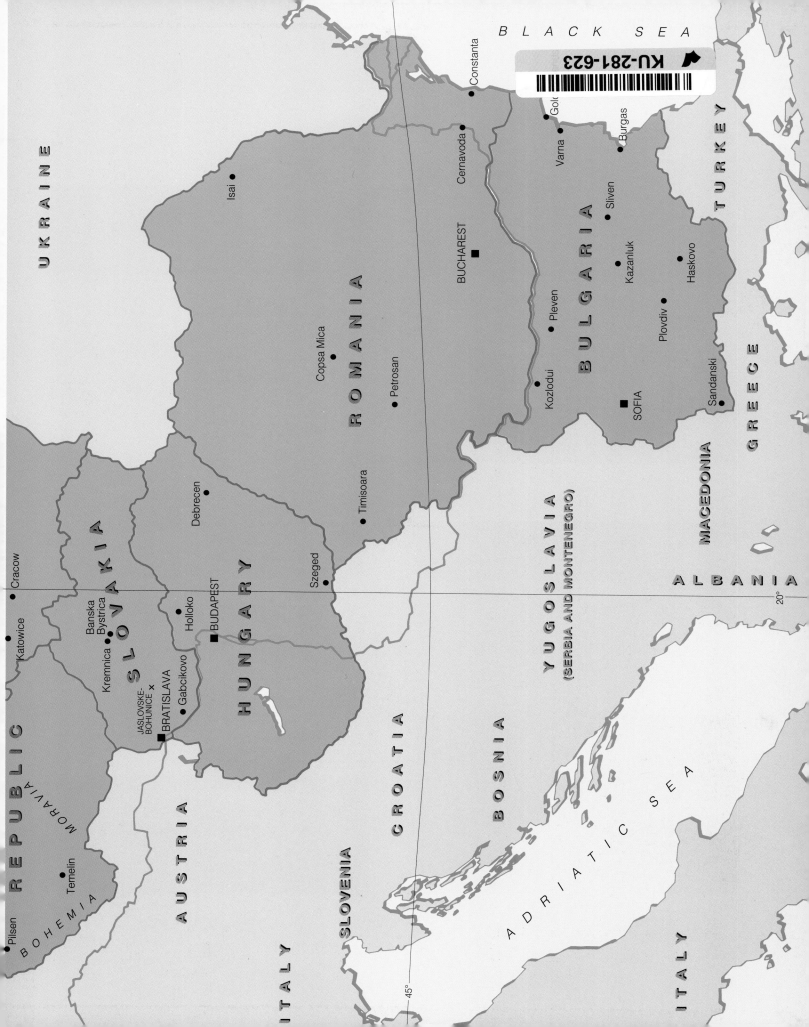

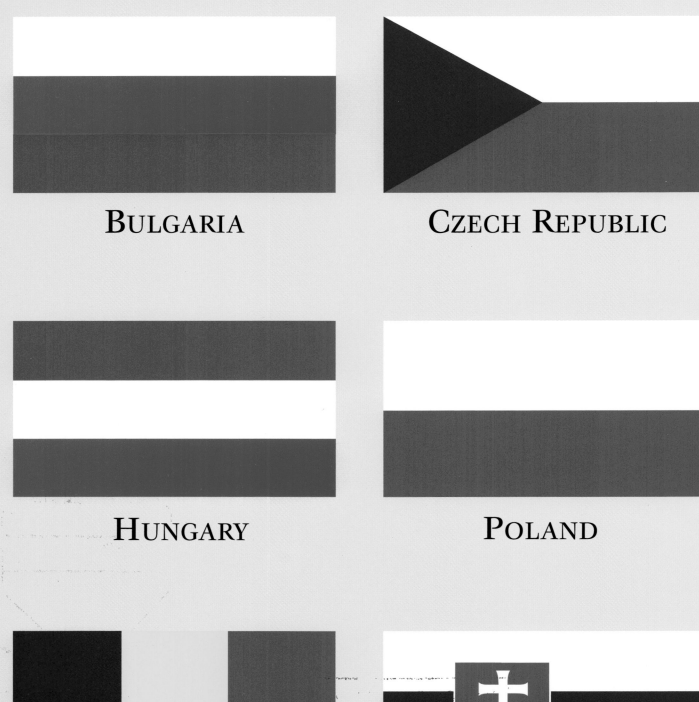

BULGARIA

CZECH REPUBLIC

HUNGARY

POLAND

ROMANIA

SLOVAKIA

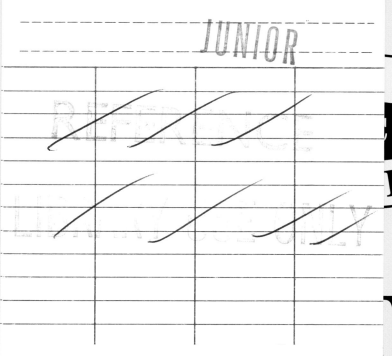

...LD
...T...ES

...TERN
OPE

Patrick Burke

MACDONALD YOUNG BOOKS

First published in 1997 by Macdonald Young Books,
an imprint of Wayland Publishers Ltd
© Wayland Publishers Ltd 1997

Macdonald Young Books
61 Western Road
Hove
East Sussex
BN3 1JD

Design and typesetting Roger Kohn Designs
Commissioning editor Debbie Fox
Editor Diana Russell
Picture research Valerie Mulcahy
Illustration János Márffy

We are grateful to the following for permission
to reproduce photographs:
Front Cover: Impact (Justin Williams) *above*;
Tony Stone Images (Joe Cornish) *below*;
Britstock IFA, page 11; Colorsport, page 25; Sue Cunningham,
pages 32, 35, 36, 43, 44, 45; The Environmental Picture
Library, pages 18 (Paul Glendell), 30 (Pilly Cowell); Robert
Harding Picture Library, pages 31 (Loraine Wilson), 39
(Michael Short), 43 (Jan Baldwin); The Hutchinson Library,
pages 19 (Carlos Freire), 25, 33 and 34 (Melanie Friend);
Impact Photos, pages 15 (Peter Arkwell), 21 (John Cole), 29
(Simon Grosset); Magnum, pages 40 (Abbas), 41 (James
Nachtwey); Panos Pictures, page 23 (Jeremy Hartley); Rex
Features, pages 9 *right* (Andras Bankuti), 9 *left* Jon Player, 12
(Lasky), 16 (Sipa Press), 20,
40 (Richard Sowersby); Skoda, page 36; Spectrum Colour
LIbrary, page 13; Tony Stone Images, pages 8 (David
Hanson), 20 (Zygmunt Nowak Solins), 38 (Gavin Hellier);
Sygma, pages 14 (Alain Nogues), 26 (J Langevin), 28 (Patrick
Forestier), 29 (Thierry Orban), 42 (G Giansanti); Topham
Picturepoint, page 17; TRIP, pages 10 (W Jacobs),
24 (J Love), (F Andreescu).

The statistics given in this book are the most up to date
available at the time of going to press

Printed in Hong Kong by Wing King Tong

A CIP catalogue record for this book is available from
the British Library

ISBN: 0 7500 2267 1

CONTENTS

Words that are explained in the glossary are printed in SMALL CAPITALS the first time they are mentioned in the text.

INTRODUCTION

Eastern Europe includes the six countries of Bulgaria, the Czech Republic, Hungary, Poland, Romania and Slovakia. The region's total population is 96,796,000 and its land area is 881,484 square kilometres: three and a half times larger than the United Kingdom and less than one-tenth the size of the United States.

Towards the end of the Second World War, in 1944–45, Eastern Europe was freed from the domination of Nazi Germany when the Soviet army moved in. The Soviet Union remained in control after the end of the war and imposed COMMUNISM on the region. For 40 years, Soviet-backed Communist regimes ruled over political systems in which no opposition parties were allowed to operate. Newspapers and broadcasting companies were controlled by the state, and most people were not allowed to travel abroad or could only do so with difficulty. In 1989, the Communist regimes were

◄ *Since 1989, Prague has once again become an elegant city. The Old Town is one of the region's most popular tourist attractions and an important source of income for the Czech Republic.*

► *For this young couple in Bucharest, a horse-drawn cart is the only affordable form of transport. Economic reforms have yet to improve the lives of many poorer Romanians.*

brought down, in popular revolutions which were mostly peaceful. In Romania, however, the uprising cost the lives of 700 people, including those of the brutal dictator Nicolae Ceausescu and his wife Elena, who were executed by a firing squad.

Today, all these states are in the middle of a slow and difficult period of change. Parliamentary DEMOCRACIES have been set up and democratically elected governments are introducing Western-style MARKET ECONOMIES.

▶ **This giant statue of a worker once towered over a street in Budapest. Now Hungarian citizens can laugh at it – and 20 other Communist statues – in an open-air museum on the edge of the city.**

EASTERN EUROPE AT A GLANCE

● Population density: 108.9 per sq km, ranging from 75.9 in Bulgaria to 123.1 in Poland
● Capital cities: Bucharest, 2.07 million; Budapest, 2 million; Warsaw, 1.64 million; Prague, 1.21 million; Sofia, 1.11 million; Bratislava: 448,785
● Highest peak: Musala, Bulgaria (2,925 metres)
● Longest river: Danube, 2,860 km in total, of which 1,600 km are in Eastern Europe
● Major languages: Polish, Romanian, Czech, Hungarian, Bulgarian, Slovak
● Major religions: Christianity (Roman Catholicism, Romanian Orthodox, Bulgarian Orthodox, Calvinist), Islam
● Major resources: Coal, natural gas, crude petroleum, copper, iron ore, salt
● Major products: Petroleum, natural gas, petroleum products, pig iron, steel, aluminium, cement, buses and cars, fertilizers, textiles and clothing, audio and electrical equipment
● Environmental problems: Industrial pollution (of air, soil and water)

The economies of the Czech Republic, Slovakia, Poland and Hungary are all growing. Signs of wealth – such as Western cars and shops, and new construction – are visible in their capital cities, Prague, Bratislava, Warsaw and Budapest. But the changes have also brought high unemployment – which officially did not exist under the old system – and new poverty. Meanwhile, the economies of Bulgaria and Romania in the south-east of the region – countries that are further away from Western markets and less attractive to Western investors – are growing more slowly.

THE LANDSCAPE

Eastern Europe extends from the Polish Baltic Sea coast in the north to the Black Sea coastlines of Romania and Bulgaria in the south-east. Three countries – the Czech Republic, Slovakia and Hungary – are landlocked. The region is bordered in the east by the states of the former Soviet Union; in the west by Germany, Austria and the states of former Yugoslavia; and in the south by Greece and Turkey.

Eastern Europe's landscape varies from plains in Poland, Hungary and on the border of Romania and Bulgaria, to the hills and mountains of the Czech Republic, Slovakia, Bulgaria and Romania. Poland lies almost wholly on the Northern European Plain – more than 75% of the country is less than 200 metres above sea level – while the Great Plain of Hungary occupies more than half of that country's land area.

Between Poland and Hungary, Slovakia

▼ *A ski-lodge and ski-jump in the Czech Tatra Mountains. Skiers use many parts of the Carpathian range, where snow can lie on the higher peaks for up to 100 days a year.*

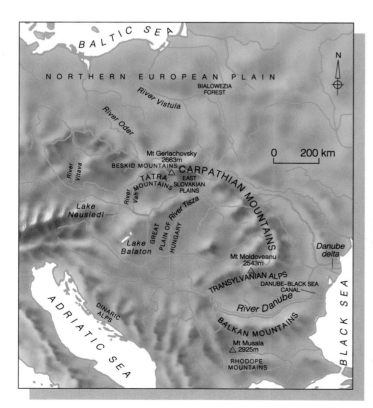

slopes down from the mountains in the north and centre to the East Slovakian plains. The Czech Republic is almost entirely surrounded by hills and mountains.

The Carpathian range stretches in a huge arc from the Beskid and Tatra Mountains on the borders of Poland, Slovakia and the Czech Republic, down to the Transylvanian Alps. Its tallest peaks, in Slovakia and Romania, are more than 2,000 metres high. About 60% of Bulgaria's land area consists of hills and mountains: the Balkan Mountains in the centre and the Rhodope Mountains in the south-west.

At 2,860 km, the Danube is Europe's second longest river, after the Volga. It rises in Germany, passes through Austria, and then flows through several other countries before it reaches Romania. Here, it empties into the Black Sea in three channels: the Chilia, the Sulina and the Sfantu Gheorghe.

Between them lies the Danube DELTA, formed 6,000 years ago. The longest river that flows wholly through the region is Poland's Vistula (1,086 km).

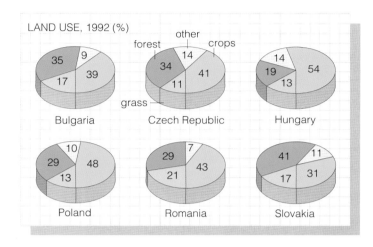

LAND USE, 1992 (%)

forest · other · crops · grass

Bulgaria: 35, 9, 39, 17

Czech Republic: 14, 34, 41, 11

Hungary: 14, 19, 54, 13

Poland: 10, 29, 48, 13

Romania: 7, 29, 43, 21

Slovakia: 11, 41, 31, 17

▼ *Over the centuries, the silt brought down the Danube has enlarged its delta into a network of channels, lakes, reed islands, pastures, woods, and sand dunes.*

CLIMATE AND WEATHER

Much of Eastern Europe has a transitional, or Central European, type of climate. It is called transitional because it shares the characteristics of two other climate types: maritime, to the west and north (including the UK and Ireland), where there is rain in all months and there are rarely great extremes of heat or cold; and continental, to the east (including Russia, eastern Belarus and northern Ukraine), where there are warm summers and cold winters. However, within this pattern there are variations, which are

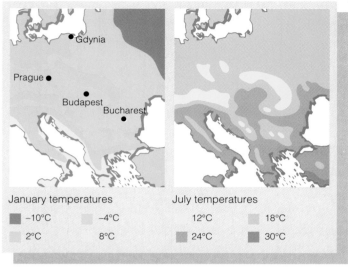

January temperatures		July temperatures	
■ –10°C	■ –4°C	■ 12°C	■ 18°C
■ 2°C	■ 8°C	■ 24°C	■ 30°C

◀ *Winter in the Polish Tatras. The highest mountains are snowbound for most of the year. Houses are designed with sharply sloping roofs to minimize the amount of snow that settles on them.*

partly caused by differences in altitude.

In the north, on Poland's Baltic coast, winter is milder than in the east and south. Snow in the Tatra and Beskid Mountains is heavy enough for winter sports to be possible. This is true of the whole Carpathian range, and on the highest peaks there is snow all the year round. The whole region can suffer severe and unpleasant weather when bitterly cold, easterly winds blow from Russia. Between 1964 and 1993, the lowest recorded winter temperature in Bucharest

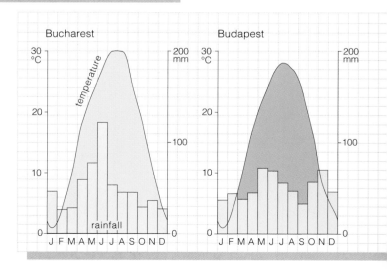

KEY FACTS

● In Hungary, spring and summer are the wettest times of the year. In early summer, almost 1 day in 3 may have a thunderstorm.
● Bucharest in July, with an average rainfall of 121 mm, is the rainiest spot in the region.

► **Golden Sands on the Black Sea was Bulgaria's first international resort. Summers here are like those in the east Mediterranean.**

was −32°C, in Warsaw −14°C and in Sofia −21°C. Inland, the Danube and other rivers often freeze over completely.

Winters tend to be a little warmer on the shores of the Black Sea in Romania and Bulgaria, with an average maximum between November and February of 6°C in Constanta (Romania) and 8°C in Varna (Bulgaria).

In the summer, the Czech Republic and Slovakia rarely experience extreme heat. Hungary's climate is affected by the position of various mountain ranges. For example, the Alps block off the moderating influence of the Atlantic Ocean. This gives the country a more extreme climate. Summer temperatures here can be high, with a maximum average between May and August of 25°C in Debrecen. In Romania, the plains in the north and east can suffer from drought as hot, dry winds blow in from the Russian steppes. Bulgaria's climate is transitional between that of the Mediterranean and the continental type, with maximum inland summer temperatures averaging 28°C.

Throughout the region, rainfall tends to be moderate.

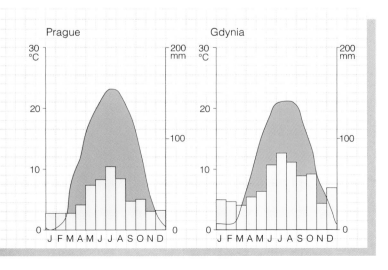

NATURAL RESOURCES

Eastern Europe has many important natural resources. Poland is Europe's largest (and the world's seventh largest) supplier of bituminous (hard) coal. Most of its estimated 65 million tonnes of reserves are in Upper Silesia. The country is also the world's fifth biggest supplier of brown coal and lignite (softer and more polluting types of coal), with the Czech Republic sixth. By contrast, the combined coal reserves of Bulgaria, Hungary, Slovakia and Romania amount to less than half of Poland's total.

Poland, Bulgaria, Hungary and Romania also have reserves of natural gas. Poland's are estimated at about 121.4 billion cubic metres; these cover about one-third of the country's demand for natural gas. Domestic production was 4,949 million cubic metres

▲ *Polish miners in Silesia. During the Communist period, the expression "Poland stands on coal" reflected the importance of coal for the country's wealth.*

▶ *A hydro-electric scheme near Sopot, on Poland's coast. Poland derives over 90% of its energy from coal-fired stations and the rest from hydro-electric stations.*

in 1993, compared with Romania's figure of 21,317 million cubic metres – more than four times as high.

Romania is the region's largest oil producer (6.7 million tonnes in 1994). It has seven offshore oil platforms in the Black Sea: these account for more than 10% of annual production of oil, gas and coal. The

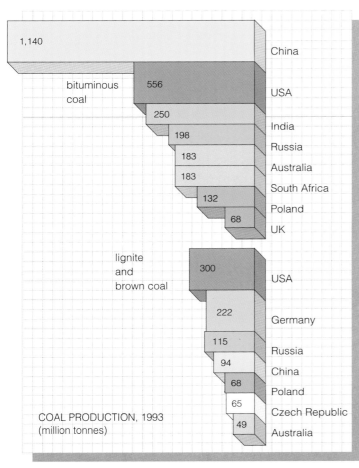

1,140 — China

bituminous coal — 556 — USA

250 — India

198 — Russia

183 — Australia

183 — South Africa

132 — Poland

68 — UK

lignite and brown coal — 300 — USA

222 — Germany

115 — Russia

94 — China

68 — Poland

65 — Czech Republic

49 — Australia

COAL PRODUCTION, 1993
(million tonnes)

annual production of oil, gas and coal. The second largest oil producer is Hungary (1.6 million tonnes in 1993). Bulgaria and Poland produce much smaller amounts, with Bulgaria's oil fields north of Varna on the Black Sea and inland near Pleven yielding only 43,000 tonnes in 1993. Although oil was discovered 80 km north of the port of Leba in 1985, Poland's oil reserves amount to an insignificant 100 million tonnes, with 158,000 tonnes of oil produced in 1992. By comparison, in 1992 the UK produced 100 million tonnes of oil and the USA 409 million.

With Greece and parts of former Yugoslavia, Hungary has the largest European reserves of bauxite, the principal ore in aluminium. Other minerals in the region include sulphur, of which Poland is Europe's second largest producer (19.3% in 1991); copper (Poland was the continent's third biggest producer in 1992, providing 12%); uranium (Czech Republic); iron ore and lead; manganese;

KEY FACTS

● Coal and coal products were Poland's second largest export item in 1994 (7.7% of the total).

● The oil fields in Romania's Carpathian and sub-Carpathian regions were once the largest in Europe, but these oil reserves are expected to be exhausted by the end of the 1990s.

● Production of bauxite in Hungary fell by 40% between 1991 and 1993, and then by another 40% between 1993 and 1994.

● The world's oldest uranium mine is in Jachymov in the Czech Republic.

zinc; and salt. Of the precious metals, gold is found in the Czech Republic, Bulgaria and Hungary, and silver in Poland.

Sources of electricity vary throughout the region. As Bulgaria has little oil, gas or high-grade coal, in 1993 around 58% of its electricity was produced by low-grade coal-fired stations, 36% by nuclear power and the rest by hydro-electricity. In Slovakia, the chief energy source for industry is

▼ *Kozlodui nuclear power station in Bulgaria. According to the International Atomic Energy Agency, it contains 2 of Eastern Europe's 6 "unsafe" or "very dangerous" nuclear power reactors.*

hydro-electric power, which is generated by a series of dams on several rivers, including the River Vah. There is also a dam on the Danube, at Gabcikovo; this began as a joint project in the late 1970s with Hungary, but Hungary withdrew from the scheme in 1992. More than 50% of Slovakia's electricity needs are provided by the nuclear power station at Jaslovske-Bohunice. Hungary also relies heavily on nuclear power.

The first of six reactors in Romania's first nuclear power station at Cernavoda comes into operation at the end of 1996; until then, coal and oil-fired plants will meet most of the country's electricity needs. Poland has no nuclear power industry.

PROPORTION OF ELECTRICITY GENERATED BY NUCLEAR POWER, 1992–94 (%)

36 Bulgaria
29 Czech Rep.
43 Hungary
0 Poland
0 Romania ★
54 Slovakia
17 UK
19 USA
77 France
34 Germany

★ Romania's first reactor comes on line at the end of 1996

POPULATION

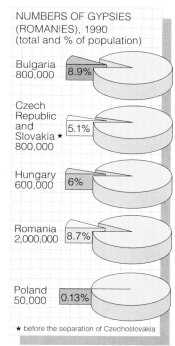

NUMBERS OF GYPSIES
(ROMANIES), 1990
(total and % of population)

Bulgaria 800,000 — 8.9%

Czech Republic and Slovakia ★ 800,000 — 5.1%

Hungary 600,000 — 6%

Romania 2,000,000 — 8.7%

Poland 50,000 — 0.13%

★ before the separation of Czechoslovakia

Population sizes in Eastern Europe vary considerably, from 38.6 million in Poland (40% of the area's total) to 5.4 million in Slovakia (5.6%).

▲ Young Gypsy girls in Romania. Eastern Europe's Gypsy population has increased by 35–40% since the mid-1970s. About half of the world's Gypsies live in the region.

ETHNIC GROUPS

In ethnic terms, the population of Poland is 98% Polish; that of Hungary 95% Hungarian; and that of the Czech Republic 96% Czech. Some of this uniformity is relatively recent. For example, in 1918, when the Czech lands and Slovakia came together to form Czechoslovakia, the new country had a rich multi-ethnic mix of Czechs, Jews, Ruthenians (who are of Ukrainian origin), Germans, Slovaks and Hungarians. But most of the Jews were murdered by the Nazis during the Second World War; the eastern part of Slovakia where the Ruthenians lived was taken into the Soviet Union after that war; the Czechoslovak government expelled 2 million Germans after 1945; and Slovaks and Hungarians left when Czechoslovakia

split into the Czech Republic and Slovakia on 1 January 1993.

There are significant ethnic minorities in Eastern Europe. The oldest and largest of these are the Gypsies (or Romanies), who have their historical roots in India and first came to south-eastern Europe in the 13th century, or even earlier. In most countries, they suffer from discrimination.

In Sliven in Bulgaria, for instance, many of the 50,000 Gypsies who make up one-quarter of the city's population live in crowded and unsanitary conditions. It is common for three or four families to live in one home and for five or six people to sleep in the same room.

There are between 250,000 and 300,000 Poles of German origin, mostly in Silesia, which until 1919 was part of Germany and

▲ *Tower blocks at Banska Bystrica, Slovakia. As in the West, large, ugly housing estates sprang up rapidly in Eastern Europe after 1945.*

still has a somewhat German character. People here often speak both Polish and German and are loyal first to Silesia, not Poland.

The second largest minority in the region are the Hungarians in Romania (about 1.6 million, or 7% of the total population). There are also 600,000 Hungarians in Slovakia. These large minorities were created when the Austro-Hungarian Empire collapsed

URBAN POPULATION, 1995 (% of total population)

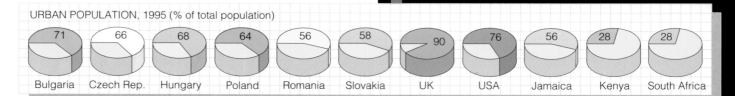

Bulgaria	Czech Rep.	Hungary	Poland	Romania	Slovakia	UK	USA	Jamaica	Kenya	South Africa
71	66	68	64	56	58	90	76	56	28	28

AGE STRUCTURE OF THE POPULATION, 1990 (% of total)

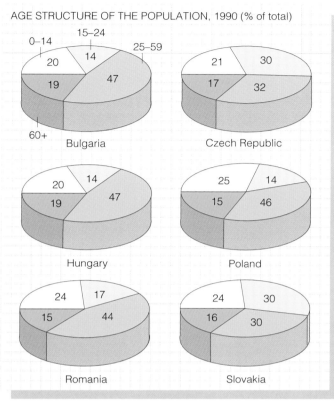

0–14
15–24
25–59
60+

Bulgaria
20 | 14 | 47 | 19

Czech Republic
21 | 30 | 17 | 32

Hungary
20 | 14 | 47 | 19

Poland
25 | 14 | 15 | 46

Romania
24 | 17 | 15 | 44

Slovakia
24 | 30 | 16 | 30

after the First World War and a new, smaller Hungary was established which left many Hungarians living in neighbouring countries. In both Romania and Slovakia, there are tensions between the governments and the Hungarian minorities. However, in March 1995 Slovakia and Hungary signed a treaty which guaranteed the rights of ethnic minorities in both countries.

URBANIZATION

In all East European countries, over half the population lives in urban areas. This is largely the result of the industrialization policies of Communist regimes in the 1950s and 1960s, which drew people from the countryside to the cities. In Bulgaria, 26% of the population lived in towns and cities in 1950; in 1970 this figure had doubled to 52% and in 1995 it stood at 71%. In

◄ *Old peasant women in the village of Holloko in northern Hungary. This house, with its cellar at street level, its whitewashed walls and its covered balcony, is typical of the area.*

◄ *Women working in the fields in Romania. The proportion of the workforce involved in agriculture fell from 75% in 1950 to 29% in 1993. Many of those living in rural areas (44% of the total) are "rural commuters" who travel to towns and cities to work.*

► *Polish farmers transporting hay. Polish peasants cultivate small plots in the way they have done for centuries. From the air, Poland looks as though it has been cut into thousands of tiny strips. The cross in the photograph testifies to the importance of the Catholic Church in Polish life.*

Hungary, 61% of people live in the industrial north of the country. In the south and east, population density is only 60 people per sq km, in contrast to the national average of 111.

POPULATION GROWTH

Poland's population has had one of the highest rates of natural increase: a rise of 54% between 1950 and 1990, compared with the European average of 31%. But by the 1990s, the populations of most countries were growing slowly, or even declining, as a result of low birth rates. In Hungary, Poland, Romania and Slovakia, an average of 37% of the population are less than 25 years old, while in the Czech Republic and Slovakia the average is 52.5%.

DAILY LIFE

The revolutions of 1989 and the removal of the Communist regimes have brought greater freedom and new prosperity for some people in the region, as well as insecurity. Newspapers and broadcasters are no longer subject to political control, people can speak as they wish in public, and travel abroad is not politically restricted. But unemployment is generally higher than in Western Europe and the USA; and the freedom to travel, for example, is available only to those who can afford it.

FAMILY LIFE

Under the Communist regimes, the family provided one of the few places where people could talk freely and relax. Today, the family still plays an important role in society, particularly in rural areas. Newly-wed couples often live with their parents or parents-in-law. However, in towns and cities more and more young people are living away from their families, and an increasing (though still small) number of young couples are living together without getting married. In Poland, the number of

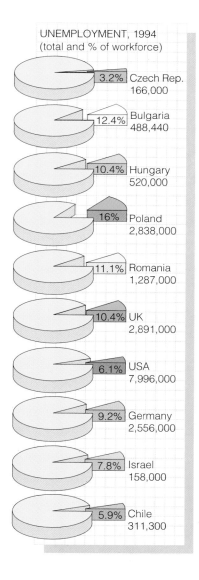

UNEMPLOYMENT, 1994
(total and % of workforce)

%	Country	Total
3.2%	Czech Rep.	166,000
12.4%	Bulgaria	488,440
10.4%	Hungary	520,000
16%	Poland	2,838,000
11.1%	Romania	1,287,000
10.4%	UK	2,891,000
6.1%	USA	7,996,000
9.2%	Germany	2,556,000
7.8%	Israel	158,000
5.9%	Chile	311,300

◀ *Miners and their families enjoying a picnic in Petrosan, Romania. A gas pipeline supplying their housing estate runs behind them. The gap between the small, increasingly wealthy minority and the rest of the population – including these miners – is growing. The low living standards of the majority are reflected in the fact that in 1994, the average household spent 62% of its income on food.*

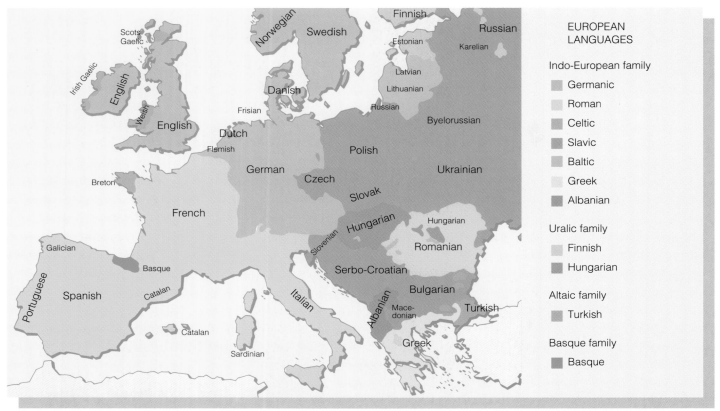

EUROPEAN LANGUAGES

Indo-European family
- Germanic
- Roman
- Celtic
- Slavic
- Baltic
- Greek
- Albanian

Uralic family
- Finnish
- Hungarian

Altaic family
- Turkish

Basque family
- Basque

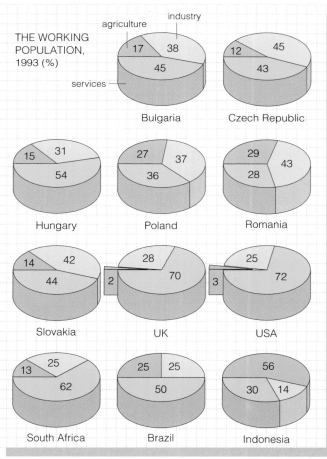

THE WORKING POPULATION, 1993 (%)

agriculture — industry — services

Bulgaria: 17, 38, 45

Czech Republic: 12, 45, 43

Hungary: 15, 31, 54

Poland: 27, 37, 36

Romania: 29, 43, 28

Slovakia: 14, 42, 44

UK: 2, 28, 70

USA: 3, 25, 72

South Africa: 13, 25, 62

Brazil: 25, 25, 50

Indonesia: 56, 14, 30

registered marriages is falling, from nine new marriages per 1,000 citizens a year in 1980 to just over five in 1995. And more children are also being born to parents who are not married. The figure has risen from 5% of all babies born in 1976 to 9% of those born in 1995.

HEALTH

East Europeans enjoy free health care, although this service is under pressure because of under-funding and high demand.

NUMBERS OF TEACHERS AND STUDENTS IN HIGHER EDUCATION, 1993–94

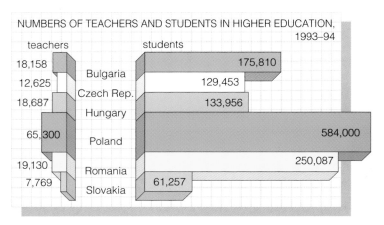

	teachers	students
Bulgaria	18,158	175,810
Czech Rep.	12,625	129,453
Hungary	18,687	133,956
Poland	65,300	584,000
Romania	19,130	250,087
Slovakia	7,769	61,257

KEY FACTS

● In 1990–95, Hungary and Romania had average infant mortality rates of 19 per 1,000 births, compared with 9 in the Czech Republic, 14 in Bulgaria and 8 in the UK and USA.

● Founded in 1348, Charles University in Prague is one of Europe's oldest universities.

● According to a World Economic Forum report of 1993, Bulgaria has an adult illiteracy rate of 8%, the highest in the Black Sea region.

● In 1989, the Roman Catholic Church in Poland was granted the right to operate its own schools. It now runs 900.

● In Hungary, there are 30,000 registered chess players who take part in competitions. Hungary is one of 6 countries whose players have won in the Chess Olympics, which have been held since 1927.

Poland and Romania provide the lowest level of health care in the region. Annual spending on health per head of population in Poland in 1995–96 was US$ 67 and in Romania $ 49, compared with $ 1,100 in France and Germany. In Romania there are 536 people per doctor and in Poland 451, compared with 311 in the Czech Republic and 320 in Germany. For the few people who can afford them, there are private medical services too.

EDUCATION

Throughout the region, schooling is free and compulsory between the ages of six or seven and 14 to 16, depending on the country. At secondary school level, pupils normally attend a general or vocational school (these emphasize practical training). A greater proportion of young people attend higher education institutes than was the case under the Communists. In Hungary, the number of students in higher education rose by 50% between 1990 and 1993. It now includes about one in eight of all young people in the country. But the proportion of those in the region who are in higher education is still only about 60% of the West European average (in the UK, about one in four young people enter higher education).

The education system has been undergoing great changes since 1989. Private and Church-run schools have been established, for example in Poland and Slovakia; and bi-lingual education is available for minorities, such as Germans and Hungarians in Romania (in spite of some continuing tensions with the majority populations and governments).

▼ *A primary school mathematics class in Warsaw. Polish children begin school in the calendar year when they have their seventh birthday.*

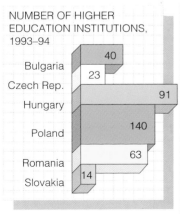

NUMBER OF HIGHER EDUCATION INSTITUTIONS, 1993–94

Bulgaria	40
Czech Rep.	23
Hungary	91
Poland	140
Romania	63
Slovakia	14

MAJOR EUROPEAN RELIGIONS

▨ Protestant		▨ Greek and Russian Orthodox	
▨ Roman Catholic		▨ Islam	

RELIGIONS

Most East Europeans are Christians, and the majority are Roman Catholics (94% of all Poles, 68% of Hungarians and 60% of Slovaks). In Bulgaria and Romania, most Christians belong to their country's Orthodox Church (83% of Romania's population, for example). Most of the region's 1.2 million Moslems live in Bulgaria. Newer Christian churches are also attracting followers: in Hungary, the evangelical movement known as "Faith" has about 100,000 members.

▼ *Rila Monastery, 120 km south of Sofia, Bulgaria. Founded in the 10th century, Rila today is both a centre of worship and a tourist site.*

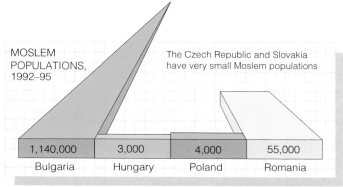

MOSLEM POPULATIONS, 1992–95

The Czech Republic and Slovakia have very small Moslem populations

1,140,000	3,000	4,000	55,000
Bulgaria	Hungary	Poland	Romania

▲ *The re-opening of a mosque in Haskovo, Bulgaria. Moslems were discriminated against under the Communists, but their position today has improved.*

MAJOR FESTIVALS AND HOLIDAYS

CHRISTIAN FESTIVALS

March/April	EASTER (all countries)
6 May	ST GEORGE'S DAY (Bulgaria)
5 July	INTRODUCTION OF CHRISTIANITY (Czech Republic and Slovakia)
15 August	ASSUMPTION OF THE VIRGIN MARY (Poland)
20 August	ST STEPHEN'S DAY (Hungary)
25 December	CHRISTMAS DAY (all countries)

MOSLEM FESTIVALS (Bulgaria)

February	SHEKER BAYRAM (Sugar Holiday), celebrating the end of the month-long fast of Ramadan
April/May	KURBAN BAYRAM (Festival of the Sacrifice), celebrating Abraham's sacrifice of a sheep in place of his son

OTHER HOLIDAYS (all countries)

1 January	NEW YEAR'S DAY
1 May	LABOUR DAY

LEISURE

Sports and exercise are still not very popular in Eastern Europe. In late 1994, nine out of ten Poles questioned in a survey said that they played no regular sport and more than half took no regular exercise. For those who did, soccer was the most popular sport, followed by volleyball and handball. Sports and fitness centres are beginning to appear, even though there are few of these and they tend to be only in big cities.

The revolutions opened up Eastern Europe to many Western influences. Satellite dishes are springing up as people tune in to Western TV stations such as Sky and RTL. In February 1994, the US company Central European Media Enterprises helped to start up Nova TV in the Czech Republic. This was Eastern Europe's first private national commercial television station. By January 1996, Nova had an average share of 70% of Czech TV viewers. Nova has the rights to show more than 6,000 foreign films and TV episodes.

▲ *Karel Poborsky (in white) scores the winning goal in the Czech Republic's 1–0 victory over Portugal in the quarter-finals of the Euro '96 football championships.*

RULE AND LAW

Since the 1989 revolutions, free elections have been held in every Eastern European country, both for parliaments and for heads of state.

The July 1989 elections in Poland were only partly free: 65% of the seats in the parliament were reserved for the Communists and their allies. But when every contested seat except for one was won by the main opposition group, Solidarity, the end of the unpopular Communist regime was in sight. The first fully free elections in Poland, Hungary and Czechoslovakia (1990–91) also produced victories for political parties that had been associated with the DISSIDENT opposition to Communism before 1989. The new Presidents of these countries had also been critics of the old system. Poland's Lech Walesa had become famous in the 1980s as the leader of the Solidarity movement and, like President Vaclav Havel in Czechoslovakia, he had served time in jail under the Communists.

By the mid-1990s, however, former Communists had been returned to power in most East European countries. For instance, the Hungarian Socialist Party (the renamed Communist party), formed a government in May 1995 with the Alliance of Free Democrats, many of whose leading members are former dissidents. In Poland, the September 1993 election produced an overwhelming victory for parties dominated by former Communists and their allies; and in 1996, the ex-Communist Alexander Kwasniewski succeeded Lech Walesa as President. In Bulgaria, where there was no strong anti-Communist opposition before

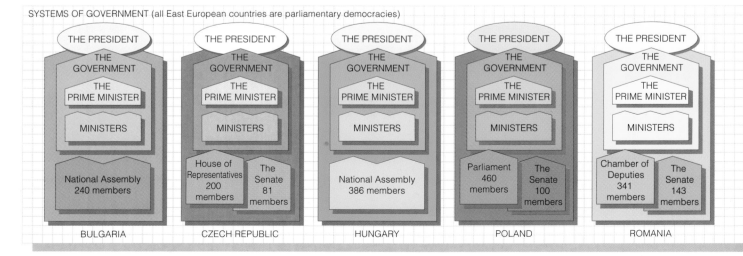

SYSTEMS OF GOVERNMENT (all East European countries are parliamentary democracies)

THE PRESIDENT	THE PRESIDENT	THE PRESIDENT	THE PRESIDENT	THE PRESIDENT
THE GOVERNMENT	THE GOVERNMENT	THE GOVERNMENT	THE GOVERNMENT	THE GOVERNMENT
THE PRIME MINISTER	THE PRIME MINISTER	THE PRIME MINISTER	THE PRIME MINISTER	THE PRIME MINISTER
MINISTERS	MINISTERS	MINISTERS	MINISTERS	MINISTERS
National Assembly 240 members	House of Representatives 200 members / The Senate 81 members	National Assembly 386 members	Parliament 460 members / The Senate 100 members	Chamber of Deputies 341 members / The Senate 143 members
BULGARIA	CZECH REPUBLIC	HUNGARY	POLAND	ROMANIA

▲ 24 November 1989: 300,000 Czechoslovak citizens crowd into Wenceslas Square in central Prague to demonstrate their opposition to the Communist regime. The largely peaceful nature of this revolution earned it the title of the "Velvet Revolution".

1989, renamed and reformed Communists have since been voted into power. By contrast, in the Czech Republic conservative political parties have been in government since the second free elections in 1992.

In some countries, the turn-out at elections has been low, sometimes close to 50%. These low figures, together with the votes for former Communists (and other left-wing parties), indicate that some people are unhappy with the consequences of the new economic reforms, or that they think politicians are unable to solve economic problems. For example, in Romania since 1990 there have been many, sometimes violent, demonstrations against price increases, low wages and unemployment.

Economic insecurity is one factor behind an increase in crime. In the Czech Republic, the murder rate has quadrupled since 1989. However, crime rates are still lower than in Western European countries and the USA.

Frustration with the new system has also encouraged old prejudices, and there is increased discrimination against ethnic and religious minorities. It is the Gypsies who are the main targets of the new racism. In 1991, there were organized attacks on these communities throughout Romania,

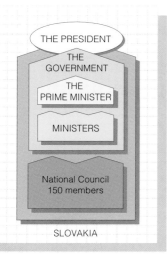

THE PRESIDENT
THE GOVERNMENT
THE PRIME MINISTER
MINISTERS
National Council 150 members

SLOVAKIA

KEY FACTS

● After his abdication in 1947, King Mihai of Romania worked as a market gardener in England, then as a test pilot and broker in Switzerland.

● In Bulgaria, the Moslem minority has its own political party: the Movement for Rights and Freedom. In the December 1994 elections, it won 15 seats in the National Assembly.

● Between 1988 and 1995, the proportion of women in national parliaments fell from 29.3% to 10% in Hungary; from 23% to 13% in Poland; and from 34% to 3% in Romania.

leading many Gypsies to emigrate to Germany. In 1992–94, Germany sent about 25,000 of them back, even though physical attacks on Gypsies in Romania were increasing.

Nationalism was an important force in the 1989 revolutions. Ordinary citizens felt they were freeing their countries from Communist regimes that were "foreign" because they were backed by the Soviet Union. Today, nationalism is still strong. The most important such development since 1989 has been the Slovak push for independence. On 1 January 1993, this ended in the disappearance of Czechoslovakia and the emergence of the Czech Republic and Slovakia.

In Romania, some people would like the monarchy back. King Mihai was forced out

▲ *A Bulgarian voting in June 1990. This election brought former Communists to power, but in December 1990 they were toppled by strikes and demonstrations.*

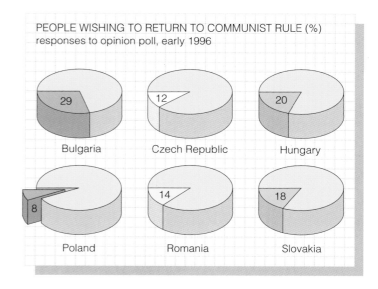

PEOPLE WISHING TO RETURN TO COMMUNIST RULE (%)
responses to opinion poll, early 1996

29 Bulgaria

12 Czech Republic

20 Hungary

8 Poland

14 Romania

18 Slovakia

◀ *Tadeusz Mazowiecki, a former dissident, became Poland's Prime Minister in August 1989. He was the region's first non-Communist Prime Minister since the 1940s.*

▼ *Soldiers in Iasi, Romania. Military service is compulsory in the region and lasts from 12 to 18 months, depending on the country.*

by the Communists in 1947. Since 1989, he has tried to return to the country several times but the government, afraid of his popularity, has refused to let him in.

Despite the hardships that many people in Eastern Europe face, there is no indication that a majority want to return to Communism. In early 1996, only an average of 17% in the region said that they wanted the old system back.

FOOD AND FARMING

Agriculture in Eastern Europe has undergone considerable change in the last few years. Before 1989, most farms were either CO-OPERATIVES or owned by the state. (The exception was Poland, where three-quarters of arable land was privately owned.)

Since 1989, much agricultural land has been privatized. In Bulgaria, private farming was legalized in 1990, and by 1994 privately owned farms supplied 72% of agricultural produce. In the Czech Republic, the figure was 90%, with private farms accounting for 85% of all arable land. One principal method of privatization has been returning land that was once confiscated by Communist governments to its former owners.

Government allowances to farmers have been cut: in Hungary by 50% in 1991; in Poland by almost 100%. At the same time, farmers have been able to sell less at home because people are poorer as a result of the economic reforms. In 1994 in the Czech Republic, farms made an overall loss of US$ 76 million because of the decline in purchases of food. Farmers are also no longer guaranteed sales in other Communist countries. And the European Union only imports a limited amount of farm products from Eastern Europe: less than 1% of European Union consumption.

As a result, agricultural production levels have dropped. In Bulgaria, total crop production fell from 9.65 million tonnes to 5.44 million between 1989 and 1993; in Slovakia, the fall was from 11.05 million to 8.23 million. And many farmworkers have become unemployed: in the Czech Republic the agricultural labour force shrank by 40% between 1990 and 1994.

If East European agriculture is to compete internationally it will have to become more efficient, raising production levels without increasing employment. In the European Union, only about one person in 20 makes a living from the land. In the UK, 2% of the workforce are employed in

◄ *Farmers ploughing a field in Poland. Like Hungary, Poland is a large exporter of food. But since the change to a market economy, it now imports more than it exports. This is because its food industry does not provide the quality that Poles now expect.*

▶ *A market in Sandanski, Bulgaria. With 110 cloudless days and 2,500 hours of sunshine a year, Sandanski is famous for its abundant fruit and vegetables. About 6% of Bulgaria's agricultural land is planted with items such as potatoes, melons and berries. In the early 1990s, exporting fresh produce to Western Europe was made very difficult by the crisis in former Yugoslavia.*

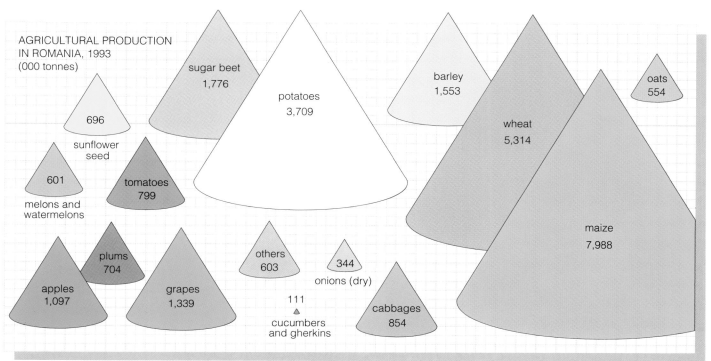

AGRICULTURAL PRODUCTION
IN ROMANIA, 1993
(000 tonnes)

sugar beet 1,776

potatoes 3,709

barley 1,553

oats 554

wheat 5,314

696

sunflower seed

601

melons and watermelons

tomatoes 799

maize 7,988

apples 1,097

plums 704

grapes 1,339

others 603

344
onions (dry)

111
cucumbers and gherkins

cabbages 854

Dried paprika on sale at an indoor market in Budapest. This is one of Hungary's best-known agricultural products.

A Budapest meat stall selling sausages. There are many types of spicy sausages, popular with both Hungarians and tourists.

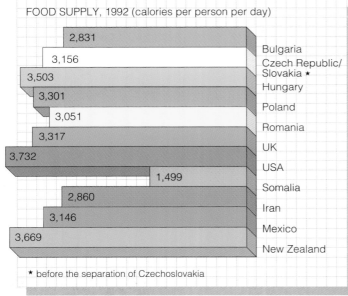

FOOD SUPPLY, 1992 (calories per person per day)

2,831	Bulgaria
3,156	Czech Republic/ Slovakia ★
3,503	Hungary
3,301	Poland
3,051	Romania
3,317	UK
3,732	USA
1,499	Somalia
2,860	Iran
3,146	Mexico
3,669	New Zealand

★ before the separation of Czechoslovakia

agriculture and they produce 2% of GROSS DOMESTIC PRODUCT (GDP): while in Poland, the figures are almost 26% (about 3.7 million people) and 7%.

Despite its grimy, industrial image, Eastern Europe is very rural. About 58% of its land area is given over to agriculture, compared with 43% in the European Union.

Agriculture accounts for an average 10% of GDP, compared with about 2.5% in the European Union.

Around 75% of farmland is used for growing crops. The principal types are cereals (wheat, maize, barley), potatoes and sugar beet.

The Czech Republic is famous for its

KEY FACTS

- The average size of a Polish farm is 7 hectares (compared with a European Union average of 16 hectares).
- In Romania, the privatization of agriculture has become bogged down in legal arguments. At the beginning of 1996, there were more than 1 million unresolved court cases involving land disputes.
- In 1993, Romania was the world's 9th largest producer of wine (800,000 tonnes), Hungary the 14th, Bulgaria the 20th, Slovakia the 28th and the Czech Republic the 34th. Top of the list was Italy (5.7 million tonnes), followed by France and Spain.
- In 1993, Poland was the world's 2nd largest producer of potatoes (36,271,000 tonnes), after Russia (38,000,000 tonnes).

hops. Known as "green gold", they give Czech beer its distinctive flavour and help make this one of the country's major products and exports.

About 25% of farmland is used for livestock: primarily pigs, poultry, cattle and sheep. Romania is Eastern Europe's largest producer of lamb and has three-fifths of the region's sheep. In Poland, poultry, pigs and cattle are the main livestock; in 1993, meat and dairy products accounted for 62% of the county's total agricultural production and 3.2% of its export income. Processed foods are also important exports. They include jams and gherkins from Bulgaria, and beetroot from Poland.

Meat and dumplings are typical dishes in Eastern Europe. A traditional Czech meal is pork, dumplings and cabbage, while Poland is famous for bigos, a casserole of sauerkraut, beef and pork. In Slovakia, thick soups known as zapraska are made with cabbage, potato, beans and mushrooms. Food in Bulgaria shows signs of Turkish influence, with kebabs and grilled meatballs part of the staple diet. Since the revolutions, Western fast foods, such as those available at McDonald's restaurants, have become increasingly popular.

People's diets are slowly changing. This is partly because economic reforms have made meat more expensive and healthy foods (such as fruit and vegetables) cheaper. In Poland, advertising has contributed to the popularity of items such as margarine that were almost unknown until 1990.

◀ *A rose-picker near Kazanluk in the Valley of the Roses, Bulgaria. Bulgaria earns US$ 30 million a year supplying 70% of the world's rose extract (attar) for the cosmetics industry. Bulgarians call roses "Bulgaria's gold". 2,000 rose petals are required for 1 gram of attar.*

TRADE AND INDUSTRY

◀ *Women bottling gherkins in Kazanluk, Bulgaria. Food and agricultural products are Bulgaria's single largest export category.*

ECONOMIC CHANGES

Since 1989, all the countries have begun to introduce Western-style market economies. The first and biggest changes came in Poland, Czechoslovakia and Hungary – the "fast-track" states. The government's role in managing the economy was reduced, and the countries were opened up to competition with the rest of the world, including Western Europe, North America and the Far East. As a result, many government employees were made redundant, some unproductive factories closed and overall production fell. In 1994, average industrial production in Eastern Europe was only 64% of the 1989 level. Unemployment also rose. In Poland, the figure stood at 1.13 million (6.3% of the workforce) in 1990. A year later, it was 2.16 million (11.8%). However, by the mid-1990s, prospects for these countries seemed to be brighter. Although unemployment was still high, it was beginning to drop or had stabilized; and the economies were growing by up to 5% each year.

By contrast, in Romania and Bulgaria, where reforms were introduced later and gradually, economic growth was slower.

EXPORTS AND OVERSEAS LINKS

The recovery in the "fast-track" states has been driven by exports, especially to Germany and elsewhere in the European Union (55–65% of the total in 1994). In 1994, their total volume of exports increased by 11.5%. Exports are important because they earn the money needed to pay for the modernization of factories and mines and for the construction of road and rail links.

Romania, and Bulgaria even more, will benefit from the new importance of the Black Sea as a trade route linking them with the former Soviet Union and oil-rich areas in the Caspian Sea, Central Asia and the Middle East. Russia, Bulgaria and Greece plan to build

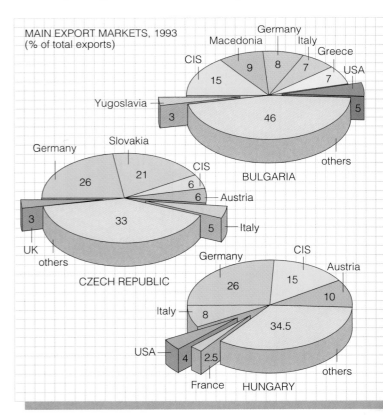

MAIN EXPORT MARKETS, 1993
(% of total exports)

BULGARIA: Germany 8, Macedonia 9, Italy 7, Greece 7, USA 7, CIS 15, Yugoslavia 3, others 46, 5

CZECH REPUBLIC: Germany 26, Slovakia 21, CIS 6, Austria 6, Italy 5, UK 3, others 33

HUNGARY: Germany 26, CIS 15, Austria 10, others 34.5, Italy 8, USA 4, France 2.5

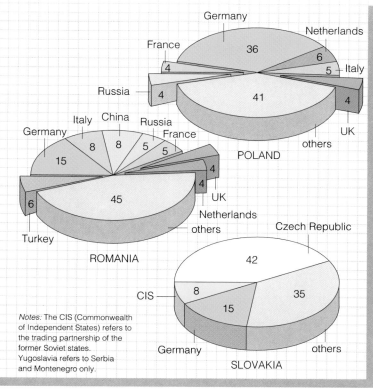

Germany

Netherlands

France

36

6

Italy

4

5

Russia

4

41

4

UK

others

POLAND

Italy China Russia

Germany

France

15

8

8

5

5

4

4

UK

45

Netherlands

6

others

Turkey

ROMANIA

Czech Republic

CIS

42

8

35

15

Germany

others

SLOVAKIA

Notes: The CIS (Commonwealth of Independent States) refers to the trading partnership of the former Soviet states. Yugoslavia refers to Serbia and Montenegro only.

▲ *A steelworks in Sofia. In 1992, Bulgaria exported 350,000 tonnes of iron and steel products. But imports of iron ore are higher: 723,000 tonnes in 1994.*

a 350-kilometre pipeline, costing US$ 700–800 million, to transport more than 40 million tonnes of Russian oil a year from Burgas in Bulgaria to Alexandroupolis in Greece.

Foreign companies have invested in Eastern Europe, for example in the form of JOINT VENTURES and new businesses. It is cheaper for them to operate in Eastern than in Western Europe. For instance, the Italian firm Fiat makes its small Cinquecento car, which is sold throughout Europe, in Poland.

For Eastern Europe, investment is good because it brings modern technology and creates access to foreign markets.

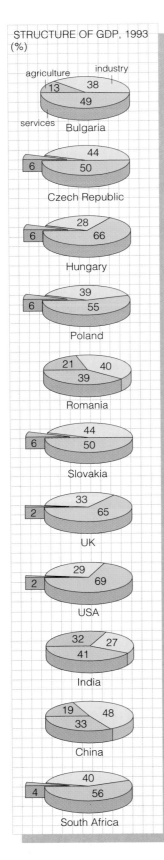

STRUCTURE OF GDP, 1993 (%)

Bulgaria
agriculture 13, industry 38, 49, services

Czech Republic
6, 44, 50

Hungary
6, 28, 66

Poland
6, 39, 55

Romania
21, 40, 39

Slovakia
6, 44, 50

UK
2, 33, 65

USA
2, 29, 69

India
32, 27, 41

China
19, 48, 33

South Africa
4, 40, 56

► *The Skoda Octavia. Skoda, the Czech Republic's leading car company, was founded in 1895. In 1991, it became part of Germany's Volkswagen group.*

▼ *Glass-blowing in northern Bohemia in the Czech Republic dates back to the 11th century. In 1995, the foreign sales of the 120 top glass manufacturers were US$ 135 million, up by 8.9% on 1994.*

MAJOR INDUSTRIES

The average size of the industrial sector was 39% in 1993 (compared with 33% in the UK and 29% in the USA). The region produces and exports everything from raw materials (Polish coal) to specialized foods (paprika and honey from Hungary). Bulgaria's main products range from cement and pig iron to cigarettes and cotton fabrics; Hungary's vary from steel to textiles and clothing, electronic goods and railway carriages. The Czech Republic is noted for its precision instruments (such as medical and dental equipment, and electronic components for

KEY FACTS

● Production of the most famous Czech beer, Budweiser, has doubled since 1991 – from 490,000 to 1 million hectolitres a year.

● About 15% of Poland's exports consist of goods and services sold to "tourists" within 100 km of the frontier. About 63% of this trade is on the German border.

● The first World Dracula Congress took place in Romania in May 1995. For a few hundred dollars, Dracula fans from the West were taken on a 5-day tour of Transylvania – the home of Vlad the Impaler, the medieval prince on whom Dracula is based.

● The Slovak Air Force charges tourists US$ 8,000 for a 4-day course where they learn to fly as passengers in a MiG-21 "Fulcrum" jet.

▼ *Rug-weaving on a handloom in Romania. Other peasant crafts here include making ceramics, and carving intricate decorations for buildings and on furniture.*

cars) and for its engineering industry. Poland's shipbuilding industry is a major source of the country's export earnings (it is the world's fifth largest producer of merchant vessels).

Smaller-scale and cottage industries in the region include glass-blowing, lace and wood-carving in the Czech Republic, and porcelain and textiles in Hungary.

TOURISM

Tourism is increasingly important in some countries. In Hungary, earnings from Western tourism in 1993 came to nearly US$ 1.2 billion, up from $ 267 million in 1985. The most popular destinations are Prague, Budapest, the Carpathian Mountains, and the Black Sea shores of Bulgaria and Romania. In 1989, 23 million foreigners visited the Czech lands; while in 1995, the Czech Republic had 98 million visitors, 45% of whom visited Prague.

TRANSPORT

During the Communist era, Eastern Europe's transport systems suffered from lack of investment. In Poland, for example, the main east–west road linking Warsaw with Berlin in Germany and Moscow in Russia still only has two lanes. The country now has plans to build 2,600 km of motorways by the year 2010; these will link up with roads coming into the country from the Czech Republic, Slovakia, Austria, Germany, Belarus, Ukraine and Russia. In Romania, a major project to improve 1,000 km of motorways and modernize border crossings was begun in 1993.

Throughout the region, trains and buses are cheap and popular forms of travel. In 1994, the UK-based National Express coach company, in co-operation with local transport firms, began running services that connect Warsaw with 17 other cities, including Cracow and Gdansk. All the region's capitals, and some other major cities, have tram systems.

Since the collapse of Communism, the demand for passenger vehicles has greatly

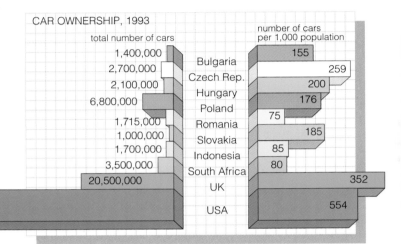

CAR OWNERSHIP, 1993

	total number of cars		number of cars per 1,000 population
Bulgaria	1,400,000		155
Czech Rep.	2,700,000		259
Hungary	2,100,000		200
Poland	6,800,000		176
Romania	1,715,000		75
Slovakia	1,000,000		185
Indonesia	1,700,000		85
South Africa	3,500,000		80
UK	20,500,000		352
USA	146,300,000		554

◀ *The Chain Bridge is the oldest of the 7 bridges that span the Danube to link Buda and Pest, the 2 halves of Hungary's capital. It was opened in 1849.*

▶ *In Prague, a tram travels the narrow streets in the Lesser Quarter beneath Castle Hill. Throughout the region, trams are cheap forms of urban transport.*

increased. Between 1989 and 1993, the number of privately owned cars rose by 19% in Bulgaria, by 21% in Hungary and by 40% in Poland, compared with increases of 4% in the UK and 2.5% in the USA. In Bulgaria, where many vehicles are second-hand, the average age of a car is 15–17 years.

The Hungarian transport system is largely based around Budapest. All main routes radiate outwards from the capital, with the result that traffic in the city is heavily congested. To the south of Budapest, there are only two bridges for vehicles across the Danube, and one for trains, which makes east–west travel very difficult.

Freight is mainly carried by road and rail. This, combined with economic growth, has produced a surge in sales of heavy trucks (those weighing more than 16 tonnes) to Eastern Europe. In 1995, sales of imported commercial vehicles in Poland rose by 57% compared with 1994 (to 3,504). It is predicted that annual sales of heavy trucks in the region will average up to 52,000 over the next 20 years.

Rivers and canals are also used to transport freight. The main shipping route is the Danube. The Danube–Rhine–Main canal in Germany makes the river part of a continuous system of transport that stretches from the North Sea to the Black Sea. The chief port on the Black Sea is Constanta in Romania. Romania and Bulgaria are both part of the 11-member Black Sea Economic Co-operation group. This was set up in 1994, and its priority is co-operation in the energy sector. On Poland's coast, Gdansk has been an important trading centre for 700 years.

KEY FACTS

● In 1993, the total road network in Eastern Europe was 431,456 km long, compared with 382,000 km in the UK alone.

● Romania's rate of car ownership (75 per 1,000 inhabitants) is the second lowest in Europe (after Albania).

● Continental Europe's first underground railway was built in Budapest in 1896. Poland's first stretch of underground (11.25 km long) opened in Warsaw in April 1995.

● Between 1949 and 1953, the construction of the Danube–Black Sea Canal in Romania cost the lives of more than 100,000 workers. It was known as the Canal of Death.

● Registered in 1923, Czech Airlines is the oldest airline in Europe.

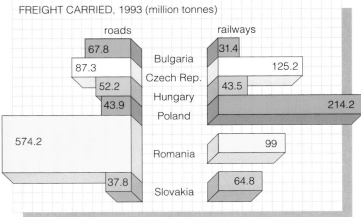

FREIGHT CARRIED, 1993 (million tonnes)

	roads	railways
Bulgaria	67.8	31.4
Czech Rep.	87.3	125.2
Hungary	52.2	43.5
Poland	43.9	214.2
Romania	574.2	99
Slovakia	37.8	64.8

▲ *The port of Constanta. The collapse of Communism in Eastern Europe in 1989 ended Soviet influence over ports such as this.*

The Danube is also a favourite travel route for tourists, who can travel by hydrofoil from Vienna in Austria to Bratislava in Slovakia or Budapest in Hungary.

Most tourists travel to Eastern Europe by car or train. Between January and September 1995, 71 million people (96.3% of the total) travelled to the Czech Republic by car or bus, 1.7 million (2.4%) by rail and 959,400 (1.3%) by plane. There are also domestic air services in all Eastern European countries.

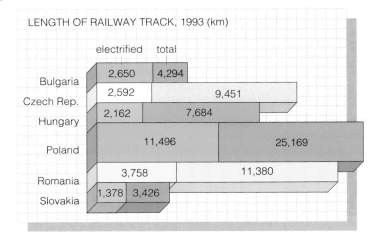

LENGTH OF RAILWAY TRACK, 1993 (km)

	electrified	total
Bulgaria	2,650	4,294
Czech Rep.	2,592	9,451
Hungary	2,162	7,684
Poland	11,496	25,169
Romania	3,758	11,380
Slovakia	1,378	3,426

▼ *A freight barge on the Danube in Slovakia. Throughout European history, the river has been an important route for trade and migration.*

THE ENVIRONMENT

Anger at the destruction of the environment and the dangerously high levels of pollution was one reason why people challenged the Communist regimes.

The pollution was caused by several factors. Power stations used low-grade fuels, such as brown (soft) coal which produces high levels of sulphur dioxide: the principal cause of acid rain. Exhaust fumes from public and private vehicles were not controlled. And large-scale industrial complexes were built without proper filtration and purification plants. The effects of these pollutants will be felt for many years.

The worst-affected area is the curve that includes south-eastern Germany (formerly southern East Germany, which was also in the Communist bloc), the north-western part of the Czech Republic, southern Poland and eastern Slovakia. Brown coal is the major culprit: for example, 75% of the Czech Republic's electricity is produced by power stations that burn this fuel. With a population of 10.4 million, the Czech Republic produces annually 13 tonnes of sulphur dioxide per square kilometre, about twice as much as the western part of Germany produces with a population of around 60 million.

More than half of Poland's 800 towns and cities have no sewage or waste-water

▶ *Children playing in polluted water at Copsa Mica, Romania. Lead-poisoning is widespread here. In 1995, it was identified as one of 24 areas in the country with intense pollution problems.*

KEY FACTS

● Nearly 3 million Poles in Upper Silesia live with up to 100 tonnes of dust per sq km annually – 4 times the maximum permitted level.

● 35–40% of Hungary's population lives with officially "inadmissible" air and water pollution. Air pollution will cost Hungary US$ 374 million in 1992–97 because of illness and premature death.

● The Carpathian Mountains in Romania are home to many wild animals: the marmot, the chamois (a wild antelope), wild boars, the mountain lynx, the brown bear and wolves.

● Europe's largest bird sanctuary opened in April 1994. Covering 142 sq km, it straddles the border between Austria and Hungary, in the area around Lake Neusiedl.

THE ENVIRONMENT

purification plants, and all waste flows untreated into the sea. The treatment plants that do exist are mostly ineffective.

Since 1990, there have been some improvements. In Bulgaria, the use of fertilizers fell from a high of 185 kg per hectare in 1985 to 45 in 1994, and the use of pesticides fell from 76.5 kg per hectare in 1985 to 16.1 in 1992. This reduction is partly due to the shrinking of the agricultural sector.

Some governments have been taking steps to combat pollution. Slovakia has introduced most of the European Union's 200 environmental directives (these cover matters such as stipulating the levels of lead in petrol, and limiting sulphur dioxide emissions from power plants). But these measures are expensive. The Romanian government has approved 102 environmental projects for 1996–99, which will cost US$ 500 million. Romania needs foreign funding to cover 40% of the cost.

◀ *A waste dump in Usti nad Labem, near the Czech border with Germany and Poland. Dumping waste is a problem throughout the region. In the early 1990s, two-thirds of the 30 million tonnes of hazardous waste that Poland generates each year were dumped in unregulated sites.*

◀ *Trees on the Polish-Czech border killed by acid rain. About 26% of Czech forests have been destroyed or damaged since 1945.*

Environmental groups play an important role in some countries. In Poland, the Polish Ecology Club, which is highly praised for its scientific expertise, is very active. There are also many local organizations, such as the Ecology Club run by the Franciscan monks.

Eastern Europe has many nature reserves and conservation areas, rich in biological resources. Access to parts or all of these areas is limited. In 1987, 9.2% of Poland consisted of protected areas; the target for the year 2000 is 15%. In Romania, the Danube delta is home to over 300 species of birds and 1,150 kinds of plants. Hungary is famous for its thermal waters, whose high mineral content has led to the development of health spas.

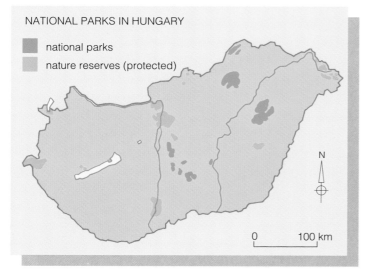

NATIONAL PARKS IN HUNGARY

- national parks
- nature reserves (protected)

N

0   100 km

▶ *One of the 250 European bison in a reserve in Bialowezia Forest, Poland – the last fragment of the ancient forest that once covered the whole of Europe.*

THE FUTURE

After the euphoria of the revolutions of 1989 and the collapse of Communism, the countries of Eastern Europe are faced with a number of challenges. High unemployment, ethnic and nationalist tensions, rising crime levels and economic insecurity all threaten to weaken popular support for the market economy and parliamentary democracy.

Eastern European governments must develop roads, railways, telecommunications systems, stock exchanges, banks, airports and power stations if their countries are to compete effectively with those in the rest of the world. For example, in 1993 Romania had only 11,600 telephone lines per 1,000 inhabitants (20% of the European average). With help from the World Bank and the European Bank for Reconstruction and Development, it has embarked on a programme to install 500,000 lines. Investment in the region from overseas is vital for development. In 1995, such investment rose to US$ 4.4 billion in Hungary (compared with $ 1.15 billion in 1993), and to $ 2.5 billion in the Czech Republic (from $ 878 million in 1994).

Western governments have an important role to play in encouraging prosperity and democracy in the region. All East European countries have applied for membership of the European Union. They argue that this would strengthen the process of economic and political reform at home. But by September 1996, the Union had not yet set a date for entry negotiations to begin.

East European states also want to join NATO, the Western military alliance. They say that this would make them more secure in the face of instability in Russia and other former Soviet states. So far (1996), NATO has only granted them membership, together with former Soviet states and others, of a loose group known as "Partnership for Peace".

Eastern Europe is undergoing a unique period of change. Despite the uncertainties, the signs are that the economic and political reforms in the region will succeed.

KEY FACTS

● In 1990–95, Hungary, Poland, the Czech Republic and Slovakia accounted for more than two-thirds of foreign investment in Eastern Europe.

● Daewoo, the South Korean car firm, controls 3 vehicle manufacturers in the region: Automobile Craiova in Romania, Avia in the Czech Republic and FS Lublin in Poland.

● In January 1996, Hungary opened its first toll road, a motorway linking Budapest with Vienna in Austria.

▲ *Volkswagen was one of the first big Western companies to set up in Eastern Europe. Its plant in Bratislava, Slovakia, is part-owned by a local company, Bratislavske Automobilove Zavody.*

▶ *The East-West Business Centre, Budapest. About 40–45% of foreign investment in Hungary is from the USA. There are more than 400 US businesses in the country.*

FURTHER INFORMATION

● BULGARIAN EMBASSY
186-188 Queen's Gate, London SW7 5HL
Provides booklets and information about, and maps of, Bulgaria.
● CZECH CENTRE
95 Great Portland Street, London W1N 5RA
Provides pamphlets and magazines about the Czech Republic, as well as maps and information.
● HUNGARIAN EMBASSY
35 Eaton Place, London SW1X 8BY
Provides maps, magazines, booklets, leaflets and information sheets about Hungary.
● POLISH EMBASSY
47 Portland Place, London W1N 3AG
Provides general and specific information sheets, as well as articles and maps, on Poland.
● ROMANIAN EMBASSY
4 Palace Green, London W8 4QD
Provides information sheets, maps and pamphlets about Romania.

● SLOVAK EMBASSY
25 Kensington Palace Gardens, London W8 4QV
Provides magazines about Slovakia, as well as maps and information booklets.

More detailed information about Eastern Europe can be obtained from the annual Country Reports *and the quarterly* Country Forecasts *published by the Economist Intelligence Unit in London and available in or through public libraries. The* Statesman's Year Book *is also a good source of information and statistics, as is the* Europa Year Book. *Both are published annually.*

BOOKS ABOUT EASTERN EUROPE
Eastern Europe: The Road to Democracy, John Bradley, Gloucester Press 1990 (age 11+)
Conflict in Eastern Europe, Bernard Harbor, Wayland 1993 (age 13+)
Revolution in Eastern Europe 1989, Patrick Burke, Wayland, 1995 (age 11+)

GLOSSARY

COMMUNISM
An economic and political system in which the state controls most of the economy and private ownership is largely abolished.

CO-OPERATIVE
An association of peasants who have pooled (or been made to pool) their land and resources for the purposes of joint cultivation.

DELTA
The triangular-shaped area at the mouth of a river where the river divides into many small branches flowing into the sea.

DEMOCRACY
A country which is ruled by the politicians elected by the people of that country.

DISSIDENT
Someone who is strongly and outspokenly opposed to the policies of a government or political party.

GROSS DOMESTIC PRODUCT
The total value of all the goods and services produced by a country in a year, except for investments abroad.

HOLOCAUST
The murder of 6 million Jews during the Second World War by the Nazi regime in Germany.

JOINT VENTURE
The setting up of a new firm by two or more private or public enterprises, for the purpose of carrying out a particular project.

MARKET ECONOMY
The economic system in which all or most businesses are owned privately, and the government does not intervene to influence supply or demand (for example, by stating what items should be produced, or by controlling prices).